Successful
Networking
in a week

*Alison Straw and
Dena Michelli*

Headway, Hodder & Stoughton

British Library Cataloguing in Publication Data

A catalogue for this title is available from
the British Library

ISBN 0 340   643412

First published 1995
Impression number 1 0 9 8 7 6 5 4 3 2 1
Year   1999 1998 1997 1996 1995

Typeset by Multiplex Techniques Ltd, St Mary Cray, Kent.
Printed in Great Britain for Hodder & Stoughton Educational,
a division of Hodder Headline Plc, 338 Euston Road, London
NW1 3BH by Redwood Books, Trowbridge, Wiltshire.

the Institute
of Management
F O U N D A T I O N

The Institute of Management (IM) is at the forefront of management development and best management practice. The Institute embraces all levels of management from students to chief executives. It provides a unique portfolio of services for all managers, enabling them to develop skills and achieve management excellence.

For information on the benefits of membership, please contact:

Department HS
Institute of Management
Cottingham Road
Corby
Northants NN17 1TT

Tel: 01536 204222
Fax: 01536 201651

This series is commissioned by the Institute of Management Foundation.

C O N T E N T S

Networking is a word firmly embedded in our vocabulary. In a week it would not be unusual to hear the word used to describe a range of qualities and activities:

They're good at networking – identifying a role model
You should develop your network – suggesting a gap
You should be logged into the network – recognising its potential

Individuals respond to the word 'network' in different ways. Whilst researching this book we have talked to many people and have found diametrically opposed views. At one extreme there are those who are vehemently opposed to networking:

I wouldn't dream of using people in such a way.
I hate asking for favours.

Others are strong supporters of networking and enjoy the benefits of a well developed network:

I couldn't exist without it.
Professionally and personally – it's a life-saver.

However you respond to the word, networks exist and can make the difference for you personally or professionally. *Successful Networking in a Week* is designed to help you understand, benefit from and develop your network.

Sunday	Networks and networking
Monday	Personal networks
Tuesday	Organisational networks
Wednesday	Professional networks
Thursday	Networking for career progression
Friday	Strategic networks
Saturday	Simple steps to networking success

Networks and networking

Traditionally, organisations have been structured as self-contained units, and those who operated within them were assigned clearly defined roles. This level of structure, definition and order meant that most internal processes were routine and understood. Today, organisations are very different. Hierarchy, definition and order have been replaced by fluid, organic organisations responding to the needs of their internal and external customers.

Jobs at all levels of an organisation are no longer defined by a set of impersonal and technical tasks. Managers' performances will be gauged by their ability to adapt, reflect and respond to these changes. Their success will be dependent on their understanding of the relationships that exist and their investment in them through networking.

Building and managing networks is not only your key to organisational success, it supports and nourishes you personally. However, as a concept, networking is in need of demystifying. In the process of understanding the concept and practice of networking, we have looked to a great many sources. The dictionary refers to a network as:

'A fabric or structure of cords or wires that cross at regular intervals and are knotted or secured at the crossings.' (Webster's Dictionary)

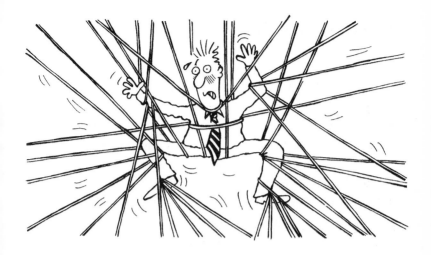

What you require from your network will undoubtedly vary. Your networking goals may be formal and structured, such as meeting peers and asking for their advice on how to achieve your career goal. Or they may be informal and unstructured such as contacting a friend and saying:

Am I going crazy?
You'll never believe what happened to me today.

Networking is not a precise science nor is it an entirely tangible range of activities or behaviours. To help you grasp a better understanding of them throughout the week, we will give you a framework which focuses on the benefits and types of network. However, today we will take an overview of networks and networking:

Networks
- Network types
- Network relationships

- Networks, what networks?

Networking
- Networking styles

Networks

If you were to take a bird's-eye view of your life and focus on your relationships and networks, it would soon become clear that they are both complex and dynamic. Networks evolve from different roots, they are established in different environments and they serve different purposes.

Network types
Our relationships evolve, in the main, through associations. These may have developed through a variety of circumstances – attending the same school or college, living in the same area or working in the same organisation. Or they may have evolved through your interests – a shared hobby, club, sport, study or voluntary work. In starting to think about networks we have identified four basic types:

Types of network
- Personal
- Organisational
- Professional
- Strategic

The relationships we establish through these networks are dynamic and reciprocal, and their boundaries are sometimes blurred. For example, relationships initially established through working together (your organisational network) often progress to friendships and, as such, become part of your personal network.

Personal networks: friends...family...chums...mates. Personal networks often emerge around a school, college, church, sports club, social centre, shared interest or activity. You choose your personal networks based on mutuality, liking and warmth. Personal networks tend to be social, they are usually developed outside the work environment and are based on an exchange of help and support.

Organisational networks: teams...project groups...committees... councils. The range of social, cultural and technological processes that have existed in the traditional hierarchical organisation are now breaking down, resulting in the devolution of power and responsibility. This promotes sharing information and co-working in order to pursue common objectives, solve problems and satisfy the expectations and needs of internal and external customers.

Team and project work are now common in today's organisations. They come without the restrictions of departments, divisions, culture or hierarchy. Teams, project groups, committees and councils all provide ideal conditions for networking. When you put together a team, you've assembled a vast and powerful network.

These networks are normally focused and developed on the basis of who you need to know to meet your objective within the time-scale. They are not based on status, but on power, knowledge and influence. A key strategy when joining a new department, division or organisation is to identify as soon as possible the organisational network and particularly those with overt and covert power and influence.

Professional networks: associates...colleagues...clients. Professional networks are built around common work interests and tasks. They can be formal networks to which you affiliate, such as institutes, societies, alumni and associations. Or they can be less formal, such as a group that develops as a result of a project and evolves into a source of expert knowledge and information.

Whilst a personal network is restricted by who you like, a professional network is constrained by what people know: their expertise. Your professional networks will no doubt change over time. You may, for example, join a professional organisation which reflects your technical specialism at the beginning of your career. As your career develops you may join other organisations which reflect your changing responsibilities, aspirations and interests.

Strategic networks: inter-organisational...externalisation... contacts...connections. The major dilemma facing organisations as we approach the millennium is that they are no longer able to meet the demands placed on them by the rapidly changing environment. Increasing competition at home and abroad, changing market conditions and rapid technological advances have created a complex and often unpredictable environment in which organisations must operate. Organisations are no longer closed systems which only look within for resources. They need to achieve 'more with less' and the only way to do this is to develop strategic networks and alliances.

It is not uncommon within organisations of all sizes and maturities to hear of reducing head count, contracting out and creating profit centres. Your organisation will undoubtedly be thinking strategically and looking to networks and alliances to penetrate and serve both local and global markets.

Network relationships
Irrespective of the types of network in which you operate, you form relationships for different reasons. The most basic reason is born of need. We are social creatures by nature and need the approval and feedback provided by relationships. However, you benefit from your networks in different ways:

Networks provide
- Information
- Development
- Support
- Influence

Information   Every manager needs information for perspective. Information in the form of data on trends, markets and opportunities can help managers plan. Information is not solely about the future; being well informed means that you can tackle situations before they occur, anticipate problems and manage situations. Action can also be influenced by information on options, strategies and possible solutions.

Development   Managers are confronted by an ever-changing environment. In this context they need to be constantly developing their skills, behaviours and processes. Development can take many forms. Traditionally, training was the route to development, but today there are many other forms of development at our disposal, for example, experts, consultants, mentors, coaches. Neglect your development at your peril.

Support   Our well-being depends on feeling supported. Perhaps we only recognise its importance when it is removed. Support can be as simple as someone showing an interest, being there, or offering guidance or practical help.

Influence   Networks can give you access to resources and political muscle. In the short term these are clearly important to your success. However, these networks can also be important to your long-term future. Identifying key people who can open doors, act as your sponsor and advocate, encourage your visibility and teach you the ropes, can make a difference to your career.

These models should provide you with the framework you require to look objectively at your network and make the necessary judgements. The key to successful networks is balance. We have heard managers say:

All my energy has been concentrated on work – I'm not sure if I still have any friends.
I seem to spend all my time supporting others – who's supporting me?

Many people concentrate their efforts on organisational networks to the detriment of their personal networks, or their network relationships become one-sided. Many networks have not been planned but have evolved and, as a result, they can sometimes become unbalanced. Networks need monitoring and reviewing to ensure that they are still serving their purpose and are of benefit.

Networks, what networks?
Networks do not exist 'as if by magic'. They develop as a result of the investment of time and energy. Unfortunately investment in one area can result in a lack of investment in another. Think about the kind of relationships you have in your networks. Do you currently have restricted access to information, development, support or influence? If so what would benefit you?

Networks evolve over time, they change shape and size according to your interests and circumstances. Ask yourself the following questions:

What do you want from your network?
Is your network serving you?
How could your network work better for you?

These are key questions and are important to ask at the beginning of the week. If you are clear about what you want, you can be precise in your networking.

Networking

The benefits of establishing and maintaining effective relationships are well documented. Most people would recognise that relationships are vitally important in all spheres of life. Your personal happiness, satisfaction and your physical well-being depend on the quality of your relationships. *Networking is all about relationships.*

Before we move on, answer the following questions:

Do you:
- Usually accept opportunities to meet new people?
- Have contacts in a wide variety of groups?
- Feel that you're generally well informed?
- Actively share information with those around you?
- Stay in close contact with your customers or clients?
- Regularly attend meetings, training courses and conferences?
- Know and talk to peers in other organisations?

If you answered 'no' to any of the above, think about the reasons why – what prevents you?

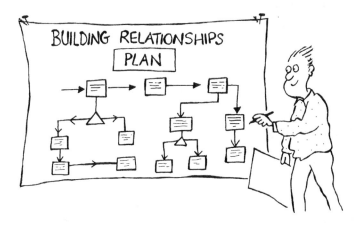

To be successful at networking you need to have an interest in building relationships and create opportunities for doing so. This can be achieved by adopting different styles. You may recognise your own style from the following model.

Networking styles

When you start on any journey you have choices. You will choose your means of transport, your preferred route and your schedule. Networking is like planning a journey. First you have to be clear about your destination and then you have choices. These choices will be dependent on:

- The time available
- How specific your destination is

You also have choices regarding your style of networking.

Styles of networking
- Conscious
- Intuitive
- Open

Conscious   Conscious networkers recognise the gaps in their networks. They identify opportunities to exploit and people to fill the gaps. This style is often used by those seeking career advancement and for developing strategic alliances.

Intuitive   Intuitive networkers are natural catalysts and enablers. Their relationships are based on mutuality and are prompted by common needs or values. Naturally, they develop strong and wide networks. However, the focus of all these networks tends to be altruistic and sometimes intuitive networkers have trouble translating their networks into something that can benefit them.

Open   Open networkers travel in a defined but general area. They invest in networks for their future potential. They develop new networks to match their interests and careers.

So, what is your natural networking style?

Summary

We began today by proposing that networks and networking could be the key to your personal happiness and professional success. If your continued happiness and success are important to you, we suggest you take this proposition seriously. Networking is not a miracle cure or a new technique which will go out of fashion. Networks are all around us. It is how we use and benefit from them that can make all the difference.

Take the time to understand:

Your networks
- Types
  - personal
  - organisational
  - professional
  - strategic
- Benefits
  - information
  - development
  - support
  - influence
- Your networking style
  - conscious
  - intuitive
  - open

Challenge yourself with questions:

What does my network look like?
How could I network more effectively?

Each day we will build on this framework.

Personal networks

You are born into a network. Personal networks are central to your early development: supporting, teaching and guiding you. As you grow older some of these functions are replaced by institutions, organisations or significant others and the importance of your natal network diminishes.

You never lose your need for personal networks as you develop; they remain as important to your well-being as they ever were in your formative years. You may, however, become distracted by other networks. We have often heard managers admitting that their personal networks are very small, mainly focused on the nuclear family and a few friends.

In the main, personal networks are based on mutuality and liking. You meet with many people throughout your life but only a few of these would be classified as friends and allowed into your personal network. You can gauge this by a number of indicators. Personal networks are made up of those whom you:

- Choose to spend time with
- Invite to your home
- Miss, if deprived of their company

Think for a moment about your personal network.

Personal networks need investment, development, nurturing and commitment. This is not a simple task. It can be more challenging to develop a personal network than any professional or organisational network because you have to build the structure. Today, we will identify methods to help you.

Recognising personal networks

There are many personal networks at your disposal.

Education
When we speak about personal networks established through education we are not solely talking about old school friends. Your school ties may have remained strong, but many find they have little in common with school friends beyond their experiences at school. It is more likely that the personal relationships you established in your later educational career will stand the test of time. The strength of

these networks is based on a shared interest in a subject, profession or shared experiences.

Work

We meet many people through work – upwards, sideways, downwards and outside:

- Bosses
- Colleagues
- Peers
- Subordinates
- Suppliers
- Customers

The proximity of the working relationship and the time you spend at work creates an environment in which close friendships and partnerships develop. Other networks develop through extracurricular activities such as a social club, sports club, interest groups, commuting together or something as informal as a drink after work.

The personal networks established through work can be powerful.

Leisure
As you develop interests you will build different networks.

> **Leisure networks**
> - Sports
> - Interests
> - Hobbies
> - Voluntary work
> - Beliefs

Shared interest and a common commitment bring you together with the people in leisure networks. The reason for meeting can become less important than the meeting itself as these networks develop. Golf clubs, Territorial Army Regiments, Photographic Societies and Political Parties are excellent opportunities for networking.

Family
It is likely that you will be influenced most strongly by your family network and how it functions. Your perspective on networks and networking will be determined by this experience. Your family networks include the nuclear family, extended family and family friends.

One of the positive facets of a family network is that members generally have the highest regard for each other. Families want the best for each other and have your well-being at heart. Referrals from family members can sometimes be the strongest and often result in real opportunities.

Personal networks are not entities that just happen. As with other networks, they can be developed to match your needs at critical points in time.

All of your existing networks have peripheral networks attached to them. If you are clear about what you want from your personal networks you will no doubt be able to develop them in accordance with your goals.

What peripheral networks are attached?
How would you like your personal networks to develop?
How can you develop them?

What you may be seeking through your personal networks are opportunities to meet with like-minded people in a non-work environment. Be clear in your needs and goals in establishing personal networks. Personal networks can provide opportunities for:

- Support
- Stimulation
- Challenge
- Appreciation
- Acceptance
- Involvement
- Enjoyment

A simple gauge to help you identify your needs is balance. It is as important to have balanced relationships as it is to have developed the right personal networks to reflect your needs.

So how do you develop these relationships?

Developing networks

Personal networks exist all around you. For many, however, these remain untapped resources, but they can serve many functions and develop in all sorts of ways. Establish personal networks by:

- Keeping in touch
- Taking the initiative
- Building bridges
- Gaining access
- Cultivating contacts

This doesn't mean being pushy. Be clear about the gaps in your networks and your needs. Think about who could introduce you into other networks which could fill the gaps in yours, or match your needs. Then start talking, meeting and building.

Nurturing networks

Networks are sensitive. If you feed networks and look after them with care and attention, you will reap the rewards.

Nurturing networks
- Be open-minded
- Keep commitments
- Do as you would be done by
- Don't be afraid to ask
- Give without exception
- Recognise problems
- Say thank you

Be open-minded
Being open-minded is the golden rule of networking. If you close your mind to the concept or the principle, it could fail. Enter new situations with a degree of optimism about what the future might hold.

Try to treat those you dislike as respectfully as those you favour. They may have just as much to offer. Often what you dislike in others is a reflection of what you dislike in yourself.

Keep commitments
When you make a commitment to do something for someone else you can never be sure of its value to them.

People tend to build their hopes around promises and commitments. By cultivating the habit of always keeping to commitments you build bridges of trust that can span amazing gaps and generate a warmth of reciprocity.

Do as you would be done by
Standards and expectations are important in building relationships. Ask yourself:

How would I expect to be treated?

Be honest in developing relationships; only nurture those you are prepared to invest in. Otherwise it can seem that you discard people when they have served their purpose. Personal integrity generates trust.

Your integrity *will* be noted by others and you *will* gather a reputation.

Don't be afraid to ask
Dependency is a value-laden term. To be told you are dependent smacks of an insult in a society such as ours which values independence. However, true independence is a nonsense, because as people we are not self-sufficient; we need relationships to perform effectively. Interdependency is a more appealing concept. We are naturally interdependent on many networks: different people, relationships and systems.

Many managers have strong networks. What they lack is the ability to benefit from them personally and professionally. It is a strength to use your networks. Ask for what you need with pride.

Give without exception

Anthropologists tell us that exchanges, assistance and giving are the most common functions of friendships in all cultures. Giving is one of the basic rules of networking.

People help each other in different ways for different reasons. This is why it can be difficult to network with those you have little in common with or even dislike. The type of help you offer is not particularly important.

You require a level of altruism to be a successful networker. You should not be possessive about giving only with a view to receiving. You will benefit at some stage of your journey but don't make doing so the only reason you network. Be careful, however, of over-giving, as an effusive networker can be a real turn-off.

Recognise problems

It may seem callous to speak of relationships, and particularly those within your personal network, as effective or ineffective. However, we would suggest that this is central.

Answer the following questions honestly, reflecting on the nature of relationships within your network.

Is your personal network effective?

Personal networks need to stay effective. They often begin as effective and that is why they are formed. But they can be corrupted by changes in circumstances, such as others coming into the network, or an unconscious change in your personal goals.

By investing in some relationships you can move them from being ineffective to effective. The strength of the tie may determine whether you choose to invest in the relationship or not. You may choose simply to distance yourself from ineffective and damaging relationships in recognition that the other party will never or could never change.

How could your personal networks become more effective? What will you do to ensure this happens?

Be sure to act; recognising problems is the first stage to managing your relationships in the future. By careful and regular monitoring you can ensure that relationship problems rarely occur.

Say thank you
If someone is helping you, let them know how much you appreciate it. If you take the time to say or do something to show your appreciation it will create an environment of continued assistance. Personal networks are often the most sensitive. You can express your appreciation in a variety of

ways. Send a newspaper cutting, an article, details of a
seminar, meeting or social event. Very little effort is
required to create a feeling of belonging.

Summary

Personal networks are easy to overlook.

The pressing needs of our busy lives can create situations
where we neglect the relationships which we benefit from
the most.

Take time to review and invest in your personal networks.

Review your personal networks
- Who do they contain?
- What are their expectations of you?
- What are your expectations of them?
- Where are the gaps?

Extend your personal networks
- Create new networks
- Select members with care
- Nurture them sensitively

Organisational networks

Traditionally, organisations were founded on the principles of hierarchy, systems and structure. They were, by character, inflexible and bureaucratic, with prescribed ways to approach tasks which now seem time-consuming and clumsy.

This is only part of the picture. On closer inspection, under the formal façade, you would discover an informal power base. Certain people are the power holders in organisations. These people are the 'hubs' of your organisational network. You are probably intuitively aware of who they are. You may or may not like them very much.

Who are the hubs within your organisation?

'Hubs' can:

Inform
- What's going on?
- How do you see it?

Influence
- Who should I talk to?
- How should I present it?

Get things done
- What are the short cuts?
- Could you see this through?

Hubs are not necessarily those with the longest service, highest status or the outward exhibitions of power. They are more likely to be natural networkers.

When you enter any new environment it is worth
identifying the hubs. Don't do this rashly – first impressions
can be misleading. Consider carefully where the informal
information and power lies. These can be identified by
making some of the following observations:

Who:
- Eats together and socialises (friends)?
- Provides solutions (experts)?
- Sources delicate information (moles)?
- Receives resources (support)?
- Is in the right place at the right time?

There is no such thing as a coincidence without a motivation.

The traditional organisations we have discussed so far today
are changing. Hierarchies are being replaced by
democracies. Status is being replaced by relationships as the
basis of power.

To be successful within any organisational culture you need
to understand the principles of networking and recognise
the power of relationships. It is these organisational
networks we will focus on today:

- Organisational structures
- The network principle
- Inter-organisational networks

Organisational structures

Just as physical structures are designed for a specific purpose or effect – rockers on rocking chairs enable them to rock, wheels on wheelbarrows enable them to roll – organisational structures can be, and are, designed for a specific purpose or effect.

Organisational structures are defined by production processes or services provision. They have characteristics that reflect different sectors, people, history, ownership, culture – the list is endless. We have chosen three common, yet different, structures for contrast:

- Flat organisations
- Hierarchical organisations
- Network organisations

Flat organisations
As a result of the recession, many organisations have stripped out layers of management. This has been necessary to meet the competitive challenges in the market and withstand the pressures of the economy.

The result of this has been that a high value has been placed on managers who not only have a functional specialism, but also have diverse experience and understand the business drivers. To complement this experience, knowledge and understanding, organisations value managers with interpersonal and communication skills, who can demonstrate competence on projects and in teams, and who have the ability to communicate effectively across various departments and business units.

Hierarchical organisations

These are the traditional, pyramid style of organisation. They usually have a Chairman or Chief Executive at the apex of the pyramid, several layers of management, increasing in number but decreasing in status as the pyramid spans out, and a bottom line layer of operators who are involved with the production of the product and who put the real value into a set of raw materials, whether these be products or services.

The method of communication in these organisations is strictly controlled. It is usually vertical (up and down the organisation), and can become blocked very easily.

Hierarchical structures encourage specialisms. Managers tend to focus on the small rather than the big picture, with limited insights across their functional borders. It creates an environment of divisions – an organisation divided rather than moving as one.

Network organisations
The new and emerging organisations of the '90s are based on
the network principle. They have changed their structure, their
styles of communication and, as a result, their performance.
Network organisations aim to combine the best of hierarchical
control and focus with lateral, cross-functional communication.

These three organisational structures are compared in
the table below:

	Flat	Hierarchical	Network
Communication	• Horizontal • Without boundaries • Between peers	• Vertical • Predefined • Within group	• Vertical/ horizontal • Encouraged • Focused
Innovation	• Flourishes • Practical problems	• Stifled • Progress blocked	• Supported • Implemented
Information	• Good flow • Lots of information	• Constipated • Controlled • Protected	• Without boundaries • Targeted
Experiences	• Limited breadth • Specialists	• Specialists • Narrow focus	• Breadth encouraged • Specialists rewarded
Behaviours	• Promotes team • Communication key	• Self-interest • Protection	• Business focus • Cope with change
Networking	• Cross-functional	• Limited	• Rewarded
Recognition	• Team achievements	• Personal success	• Team and personal

The network principle

- Essential characteristics
- Establishing the culture
- Barriers to change
- Unblocking organisations

Essential characteristics
Network organisations have advantages, not solely because of their internal characteristics, but because of their ability to compete.

Essential characteristics:
- Innovative
- Flexible
- Fast-footed

Innovative   Innovation is the key to survival in the highly competitive environments in which organisations exist today. Truly innovative organisations encourage creativity at all levels.

In hierarchical organisations, ideas tend to be passed from one person to another rather like a baton in a relay race. If there is a weak link in the chain, the idea goes no further and creativity is quashed.

For an organisation to innovate successfully, it is important that functional specialists network between themselves. This network is one in which ideas are encouraged. If they are good they fan out, get picked up and are reinforced from many different perspectives.

Innovation through networks:
- Encourages
- Refines
- Reinforces
- Recreates
- Implements new ideas

The culture and structure to support this innovation is characterised by open channels of communication which encourage and reward an enthusiastic exchange of ideas across functional boundaries.

Flexible   This style of organisation demands new skills of managers and team members. Managers have to broaden their skills to become more effective as:

- Team members
- Catalysts
- Communicators
- Enablers
- Informers
- Project managers

Proprietorial styles of management are not helpful in this environment.

The skills listed above are typically practised in the following environments:

- Cross-functional teams
- Briefings
- Brainstorming groups

- Continuous improvement groups
- Quality circles

Managers who thrive in these environments adapt well, and are not threatened either by change or by the unknown.

Fast-footed   Fast-footed organisations are those that are able to respond rapidly to changes in the demands placed upon them from:

- Employees
- Customers
- Suppliers
- Community
- Environment

The success of this response leads to prosperity and growth. There is no substitute for keeping your ear close to the ground, hearing and acting upon new ideas and developing trends.

Organisational structures have to be able to withstand the
pressures of these new demands. If they are too brittle, or
too inflexible, they will shatter. Flatter structures and
networks will assist organisations in the process of
toughening up, and of developing resilience.

Establishing the culture
Regardless of the dominant style of your organisation, there
will be aspects of it that you will wish to retain and those
that need revising. Unless there is a crisis in your industry
or your organisation, the adjustments that need to be made
in order to become network orientated need not be
dramatic. Indeed, it may take some time to encourage
people to change their behaviour. However, with constant
reminders, reinforcement and reward, this can be
accelerated.

When trying to establish a network culture, employees will
need to know exactly what the organisation is trying to
achieve. Messages must come down from the top and be
reinforced time and again. Senior managers must be seen to
practise what they preach.

If you occupy a 'secure' position in a traditionally
hierarchical organisation, networking may seem self-
defeating. Sharing information may be perceived as giving
power away. However, it is a two-way process and can, in
the right conditions, enrich everyone.

But first, the conditions in which new behaviours can
emerge must be put in place. These will only take root if
everyone understands the initiative and can see its value.
The following imperatives will help to fuel change:

- Recognise individual and the team contributions
- Encourage career paths across functional boundaries
- Remove functional focus from analysis
- Instil discipline of broader perspective
- Encourage cross-functional communication
- Share organisational information
- Support change with training and development
- Monitor and evaluate

You are essentially capitalising on the expertise contained within the organisation. This involves recognition and action. Try some simple steps, such as building project teams across functional boundaries, introducing network mentors, identifying behavioural role models, offering counselling and support. Create opportunities that will naturally encourage networking: continuous improvement groups, quality forums, brainstorming activities, work exchange schemes and social functions.

Network organisations are not constrained by the limits of the organisation. They look outside for examples of good practice, innovation and success. Look beyond *your* organisation at:

- Competitors (benchmarking)
- Customers
- Suppliers
- Professional bodies
- Conferences
- Placements
- Research
- Joint projects

In multinational organisations, additional mechanisms will be required to facilitate communication across national borders. Such mechanisms could include:

- Electronic mail
- Teleconferencing
- Exchange visits
- International training
- Newsletters
- International conferences
- Internet

Networking should be encouraged between *opposite numbers* in the organisation and these *opposite number* networks should be tapped too.

Barriers to change
There are a number of different stumbling blocks that prevent effective and efficient networking. These come in the following forms:

- Inertia
- Fear
- Ignorance

Inertia   Inertia is often found in organisations that do not place a high importance on networking. These will be of the more traditional type that believe networking is idle gossip and has no value. Actually, idle gossip often does have value, but that is another matter!

Fear   Fear stems from the belief that control will be lost and that those who don't believe in networking will sabotage all efforts to change the culture. Control is an interesting issue. If too much of it is exerted, people identify subversive techniques to get round it. This results in a two-tier culture, the overt and the covert, and is in direct opposition to the culture of a networking organisation. Too little control, on the other hand, results in frustration and a loss of respect for those who occupy the positions where control is expected of them. A firm but receptive approach is generally the most effective.

Fear is exhibited in different ways: in retrenchment, lack of cooperation and possessiveness of information or power. Organisations are sometimes peppered with those who do not want to share information: 'functional primadonnas'. They believe in the vertical separation of functions and discourage lateral communication. Their catch-phrases might be:

Mind your own business.
Stick to what you know.

Ignorance   Many people do not possess natural networking skills so these must be developed and encouraged so that the new culture has a good chance of becoming established.

Often people think that the only component of networking is technology. This is merely a tool, it is not a network in its own sense. Networking is about human interactions. These interactions can be facilitated through communication technology, but never replaced by it.

People in organisations hold a lot of experience and many skills which are not well advertised. Some of them are related to their professional role, others are personal. It is amazing what talents you can unearth when you network.

Unblocking organisations
Variety is exciting, creative and dynamic and needs to be celebrated. Recognition of transferable skills and qualities needs to be expressed in a way that will mobilise the workforce and motivate people to network and give more. If a match can be made between individual and organisational objectives, all the activities that take place within the workplace will contribute towards the achievement of strategic goals.

The secrets behind a successful shift to a networking culture are the four **C**s:

- **C**ommitment from the top
- **C**onstant reinforcement
- **C**onsistency
- **Communication**

There is never enough of the latter activity, so do it once, do it again and do it again.

Inter-organisational networks

Organisations can benefit greatly through careful strategic positioning in relation to other organisations' products and services. What attracts a customer to another product or service could equally well attract a customer to your own. Washing-machine manufacturers have, for years, struck up beneficial relationships with washing powder manufacturers. One carries the recommendation of the other – they go hand in hand – and together, they aim for the same target market with more force and precision than they could do alone.

These synergistic relationships now extend beyond the mere marrying of products to the physical positioning of company outlets. With the mushrooming of industrial estates and out-of-town shopping centres, many such relationships exist. It is almost inconceivable that a Showcase Cinema does not occupy the same site as a McDonald's or Pizza Hut. Equally, DIY stores such as Texas, Charlie Brown's and Do-it-All are often found together.

Customers are much more inclined to make the journey out of town if many objectives can be achieved in one fell swoop – and if entertainment is thrown in for good measure.

Popular combinations of consumer outlets will be well known to you:

- Pizza Hut + Showcase Cinemas + Rank Bowling
- MFI + Texas + Charlie Brown's + Carpet Right
- M&S + Next + Leatherworld + Habitat + Toys ' Я ' Us

The same is true of the high street, of course, and has been for many years. All the well-known high street shops such as Boots, W H Smith, Marks and Spencer, situated conveniently together, hold a tremendous allure for the shopper. Gone are the days when browsing was a pleasure and time was an inexhaustible supply.

Summary

Organisations dominate our life. It is better to understand them, adapt and benefit from them, than clash. Understand and recognise the structure of your organisation. Then, decide if a change is necessary and if so, what it is appropriate to change: you or the organisation.

Organisational networks check-list
- Recognise
  - hubs
  - structures
  - characteristics
  - resistance
- Change
  - behaviours
  - culture
  - expectations

Professional networks

Professional networks assist you in your professional progression. They can provide information, support, influence and development. Above all they are a vehicle through which you can identify and create opportunities.

> *Professional progression*
> - Information
>   - What is the best strategy?
>   - Who is the expert?
> - Support
>   - How do you see it?
>   - How would you feel?
> - Influence
>   - Who should I be talking to?
>   - Can you introduce me?
> - Development
>   - How can I get up to speed?
>   - What do I need to beware of?
>   - How can I find out what I don't know?

Professional networks are built around common work interests and tasks. Your organisational network is likely to be a subset of your professional network. However, professional networks can consume other networks to which you affiliate, such as institutes, societies, alumni and associations.

Professional networks have no bounds: they extend right around the globe. As a professional, you have licence to tap into the network in the natural course of carrying out your professional duties or on the wing of a business proposition or idea. Indeed, it is an approach such as this that will lead to the creation of profitable alliances and the building of business opportunities. Today, we will guide you through this process:

> *Professional networks*
> - Where are they?
> - It's a small world
> - Building bridges
> - Feed and water regularly

Where are they?

For simplicity, professional networks have been divided into various categories: intra- and extra-organisational, professional organisations and electronic networks. The various forms of professional network have different codes of conduct so it is useful to consider these and try to determine what they may be.

Intra-organisational

- Colleagues
- Peers
- Superiors
- Bosses
- Grapevine
- Political
- Personal alliances

The code of conduct for making connections in the work environment are fairly well defined from a professional standpoint. Knowing and understanding the undercurrents that create the political tenor, however, are key to your success in working the organisational network effectively. These invisible influences and patterns need to be observed and considered from a safe distance.

Bide your time. Only when you feel secure that you have correctly identified the various allegiances and loyalties that exist in the organisation is it time to form your own alliances. Don't rush in where angels fear to tread. Others' perceptions of you will be coloured by those you fraternize with. *Mud sticks by association.*

Although you are more or less bound to fall into a political minefield at some stage, persevere – you will soon learn to trust your observations and, with your successes, develop faith in your instincts.

Extra-organisational

- Competitors
- Customers
- Suppliers
- Agents
- Partners
- Alliances
- Family and friends
- Past colleagues
- College/university contacts
- Alumni groups

When engaging with those outside your working environment you will need to be aware that *all* your communications and actions will go towards creating an impression of your organisation and of your own professional integrity. Mismanage this at your peril. It is amazing what a small world it is. You will find that people you connect with outside your organisation often have a feeder back into it, through a different channel.

People have a need to judge and they will use whatever material is available on which to base their judgements. If you put a foot wrong in the initial stages of your relationship, usually within the first few seconds of meeting, it will determine the dominant impression that the other party has of you. Recreating or altering an impression is disproportionately harder than creating one in the first place.

Professional network organisations

- Professional bodies
- Clubs
- Political parties

Many network organisations now exist. They are designed to facilitate networking amongst those with similar interests, values, professions and predispositions. Some of these organisations are open and welcoming of new members, others are closed. Barriers such as gender, race, social standing and profession are observed in some organisations.

The vehicles of communication for activating a network are things such as: regular meetings, seminars, workshops, group activities, social events, and so forth. Although not everyone's cup of tea, they are extremely useful ways of contacting a target group of others who are highly likely to want to connect with you – professionally or personally.

Professional networks include:

- The Institute of Management
- Chartered Institute of Marketing
- Institute of Personnel and Development

Electronic networks

Electronic networks such as Local and Wide Area Networks, Super Janet and the Internet were heralded as the technological answer to the rapid and efficient exchange of information. These established and developing networks are transforming organisations. They give organisations access to high-quality, up-to-date information which, in turn, enables sound and relevant decision-making.

Dependency on electronic systems, however, can have its limitations. It cannot replace the benefits of defining and discussing problems and solutions, building a shared understanding of the situation, discussing shifting priorities and the socialisation function of networks. It also prevents the interpretation of non-verbal signals.

It's a small world

A good professional network can support you in your:

- Role
- Career
- Personal life

Your role Everyone requires professional checks on their role and performance. Networks can provide you with this in a variety of ways:

- Feedback
- Know-how
- Benchmarking
- Management information
- Problem-solving
- Challenge

Your professional network can act as your safety net, i.e. providing opportunities to share practice, thoughts and opinions in an environment that is not constrained by the knowledge and experience of the organisation.

Professional networks ensure that you keep up to date. They are the mechanism through which you can access information, knowledge, ideas and insights into the latest thinking of professional significance. In addition to information they are sources of expert knowledge and advice. They provide an environment in which you can learn from others who have already encountered situations that are new to you.

Some form of self and role evaluation is essential for all professionals. It provides professional standards, levels of competence and targets against which you can judge yourself and through which you can identify your development needs. Every professional should take responsibility for their own continuous professional development. Professional networks give contacts which enable you to benchmark yourself. Beware of the ethical issues around insider knowledge.

Your career   Your professional responsibility extends beyond your need for continuous development in your role to responsibility for your career.

Professional career benefits:
- Feedback
- Assistance
- Exposure
- Early warning

Professional networks are unique in that they can offer open and objective opportunities for feedback. In this way you can develop an understanding of how you are perceived by others in a professional arena. Used wisely networks can offer professional visibility, exposure and lead to real opportunities. On Thursday, we will give you more insights into networking for career progression.

Your personal life   Professional networks can support you in a variety of ways.

Personal benefits:
- Spawning social circles
- Recommendations
- Referrals

Social circles are often created as a result of networking in the professional arena. These will transcend the professional networks from which they came. If this happens, it is a bonus. However, be alert to the confusion that can arise around the liberties friends can take against those professional colleagues can take. It would be hard for your boss – and perhaps for you – if you asked for a babysitting favour, for example!

Building bridges

Networks can emerge and disappear like Brigadoon. They can be created in order to meet a specific goal and dissolved once this goal has been met.

When a temporary network is required, it needs to be carefully mapped, monitored and evaluated. After its dissolution, some of the good contacts that you have made may be preserved for placement in another of your networks.

In order to make the most of the potential a network holds, it is important to be clear about what you want from it.

What do you want from your network?
- A new position
- News of tenders
- Entry to an inner circle

By identifying what you want from your network, you will be clear about selecting its members.

Feed and water regularly

A network is only as good as the care and attention you give it. This is not necessarily a time-consuming activity – it becomes almost instinctive although your networks will need general maintenance on a regular basis.

Maintain your network by:

- Pruning
- Growing
- Investing
- Rewarding

Pruning
It is likely that at any one time you have relationships in your network that no longer serve or benefit you. These relationships can sap your energy and divert your focus unless they are pruned.

Growing

Consciously and consistently add to your network. Be very clear of your goals though and be sure of the key players and their allegiance to you. It is very easy to muddy your own waters by wasting the potential of a good contact.

Investing

Keeping a network alive and active requires an investment of time and energy. Take care to be sensitive and courteous. It would be a shame to milk the network too much and lose your credibility and the goodwill others have for you.

Rewarding

Don't forget to thank those who have assisted you. Aftercare is as important as maintenance.

Summary

Professional networks can be powerful mechanisms if you are clear about:

What you want from them.
How to make them work for your benefit.

To demonstrate their breadth and potential:

1   Select a high-profile name – Sir Adrian Cadbury, Professor Charles Handy, John Hobson and try to identify how many people in your professional network you would need to approach in order to make contact with your chosen subject.

2   You may, of course, already have some superb contacts in your network. Try thinking about your

network from a different vantage point and see if you can identify where these contacts could lead you.

Professional networks check-list
- Identify networks
  - intra-organisational
  - extra-organisational
  - professional
- Clarify goals
- Build relationships
- Monitor, manage and review

Networking is never one-way. To support the existence of professional networks you will need to play your part in serving them.

Networking for career progression

The concept of networking has its origins in the context of careers. Most people at some stage in their career will have used their network to aid their progression. Your first job, Saturday job or summer jobs may have come about because of a contact your parents, family or friends had. When older, you develop a more sophisticated version of this as your network extends beyond your personal networks.

Think about your career:

How did you hear about the jobs?
How did the recruiter hear about you?

This traditional and well-tested means of developing and progressing your career is even more important now that organisations are flatter, allowing fewer opportunities for upward promotion. In these new organisations the way people group together is far more fluid. This has consequences for the traditional management career and the expectations that many managers hold about their futures.

Traditionally, managers had certain expectations about their careers, which were based on the pyramid structure of organisations. When you entered an organisation, the career structure was such that you could be clear about your end point and the time-scale involved.

These days successful careers are based on networking, not on a traditional career path carved in stone. Knowing how to network to progress your career is an essential survival skill. To survive means using your career networks responsibly and ethically.

You should take responsibility for your career and *make* your luck by investing time, energy and money to ensure that your career goal in the short, medium and long term is achievable. This responsibility is as important if you intend to stay with one organisation as it is if you intend to move. To devolve the responsibility for your career onto any organisation is to neglect it.

Today, we will help you think about careers and how to develop your network to benefit you professionally:

Networking for career progression
- Begin with the end in mind
- It's who you know
- What to say after you've said hello

Begin with the end in mind

If we were to pose a simple question to you such as, 'who are you?' we would not be surprised if you hesitated and began by answering, 'I'm an Operations Manager' or 'I'm a Training Manager'. We tend to think of ourselves as what we do, rather than who we are. This can have its dangers. In the past, as a result of the changing needs of the organisations in which we worked, we probably became what was demanded of us with little thought or reflection about what we enjoyed or what we did best.

A successful career is made up of many components: job type, style and content, development, fulfilment and fit. Getting this right is dependent on understanding yourself. What are your:

- Skills
- Strengths
- Limitations
- Values
- Interests
- Pleasures
- Achievements?

Do not focus only on your education, skills and experience to formulate your next move. Focus on what makes you different and unique, and how you could contribute to an organisation. Also focus on what you enjoy, what gives you a buzz. Natural enthusiasm is easily conveyed and extremely contagious. Opportunities are in short supply and competition is fierce. It is essential that you communicate your value and create a good impression.

Where do you want to get to?
Having taken an honest and thorough look at yourself, how clear are you about where you want to get to – your destination? Whilst your future may seem hazy, some idea of where you're going helps you plan your moves and gauge your progress.

Where you want to get to can have many stages; perhaps the simplest way to think of these are as your short-, medium- and long-term goals.

Some people have goals that are not work-related, but do impact on their work. One manager we met had the goal of retiring at 50 in order that he could concentrate on his interests. This directly affected his career and his career choice because he needed to achieve a level of income to support him in his ambition. Others have goals such as embarking on a second career. In this case, they will need to invest in the networks to ensure that this is realised.

In the short to medium term your goals may be related to more tangible things such as:

- Location
- Function
- Sector
- Rewards
- Work style
- Colleagues
- Organisation

Goals need reviewing regularly, as they might be unrealistic and over- or under-ambitious. The rapidly changing business environment and the high level of uncertainty can significantly affect our goals. Over time, goals can change as we develop.

Begin with the end in mind! This end can then be built into your daily life so that you can manage yourself each day to be and to do what really matters most. Every decision you make will be in the context of your goal so by definition you will be inexorably moving towards it. This in turn helps you to target your network. Your targets could be triggered by:

- Contacts in your preferred locality
- Role models
- Functional experts
- Hubs in your sector

It's who you know

Your current contacts are the raw material for the job search.

They in turn have contacts of their own. What you have at your disposal now is an enormous network.

Who do you know?
As a start, organise this raw material into a database of contacts. The format of this doesn't matter – index files, personal files, computerised records – whatever suits your style. Include the following information:

- Person's name
- Title, position
- Name of company
- Phone and fax numbers
- Address
- How you know this person
- Date of contact
- Result of contact
- Dates and action for follow-up

Even if you love your job and have no intention of moving at the moment it would be good to start your database now. The perfect time to organise and develop your network is when you don't need it.

This networking process is gradual. It is an investment in the development of a sequence of personal contacts that can potentially move you towards your long-term career goal. The first step in targeted networking of this nature is to identify holes in your network. Are there gaps between your current job and your targeted job?

Maybe you already have contacts in the department, division, organisation or industry that you have targeted or maybe you need to find a point of entry.

You are aiming to establish a network made up of contacts who serve you in one of the following ways:

Your contact:
- Sees a job advertisement
- Hears information about a local organisation
- Knows a recruiter who specialises in your function
- Knows someone with influence or information
- Identifies a vacancy within their organisation
- Offers you a position

A quality contact could be someone in a position to offer you a job or arrange an interview, but potentially you are looking for anyone who has a pair of eyes or ears.

You cannot always be in the right place at the right time, but by developing your network you have more of a chance of hearing about, seeing or recognising the right opportunities.

With your goal in mind, it is important to think about who can help. It is often the people you have the weakest links with, your old contacts that have lain dormant for years and have almost been forgotten, that can be the most effective in your career progression. Weak links can provide you with new information and the essential bridges to other groups and networks. Your strongest links would tend to be functioning well already so they will only need reminding of your requirements.

Who can you get to know?
You may also need to extend your network and you can do this through using:

- Yearbooks
- College alumni
- Conference attendees
- Company phone directories
- Committee and team assignments
- Trade or professional associations
- Sponsorship into other networks

Career visibility
Mobility is the key to network building as this can lead to visibility. Make and take every opportunity to move into new networks. Explore new:

- Venues
- Places
- People
- Opportunities

Volunteer to take temporary assignments with another group, division or subsidiary. Join new committees and teams, especially those with representatives from other departments in your organisation. Attend and participate in business and social events.

Network building through:
- Outside meetings
- Conferences
- Seminars
- Professional institute events
- Trade shows

Remember the point of this visibility exercise is to meet different people who bridge different business and social circles. You may also want to try local events such as a village or town meeting, parent–teacher association, lectures or any other event where you can naturally meet other people.

For the rest of the week, note down in your diary all the people you meet during the course of each day. Indicate the networking potential of each contact.

What to say after you've said 'hello'

Be aware of the people you need in your network. Always remember this as your target and plan your networks. You need to ask yourself repeatedly, 'How can I meet the people I need to?'

It is one thing meeting these people, but quite another being able to benefit from the meeting. This is often the point at which many people fall; they have extensive networks but are not skilled at using them.

Think carefully about how you build productive relationships and how to establish rapport.

Building blocks
- Sponsor's recommendation
- Reputation of the individual or organisation
- Well-known accomplishment
- Position in the community
- Mutuality
  - an issue you share
  - an organisation you belong to
  - work or life experience

Prove you are worth talking to; prepare a short summary of your career. Make it positive and base it on recent and relevant achievements. Be succinct and deliver it with energy and enthusiasm. Also state your career goal.

How can they help?

It is important to communicate how they can help. Their support could be invaluable and information is always useful.

Information
- Is the business expanding or shrinking?
- What companies are doing well?
- What developments are current or planned?
- Who are the key people who make recruitment decisions?
- What opportunities are available?
- Salary levels

Support
- Comments on your curriculum vitae
- Advice on approaches
- Opening doors
- Advice on presentation at interview

Some people will simply be too busy to spend time with you. But they may also know others who can help. Always end with the phrase:

Who else should I be talking to?

This is the point at which you are building the bridges between different circles.

If you are asking for an introduction, be aware of what the other person thinks of you. If they have any doubts about your abilities they may not be the best person to use.

Script and rehearse what you intend to say. Practice makes perfect. You don't get a second chance to make a first impression.

If someone has taken the time to meet with you, keep them up to date. If you have followed their advice, tell them of your progress. If they haven't heard from you for some time they will tend to assume the best – that you have been successful in your quest.

Summary

Successful people know that the way to opportunities and advancement can come from a network that is carefully maintained.

Networking for career progression check-list
- Know yourself
- Communicate your career goals
- Nurture contacts
- Follow up

The value of networking is that you are constantly advertising yourself. You are making your luck by:

Being in the right place at the right time.
Knowing the right people.

Strategic networks

So far this week we have looked at networks from different vantage points. The consistent themes have been how they could benefit, support and develop you personally and professionally. Today, we change our focus and identify how networks can benefit and support organisational development. We will focus on:

- International networks
- Strategic networks

International networks

International networks stretch out across the globe and embrace many cultures. They are not exclusively manufacturing or retail operations, they include apolitical, non-denominational, humanitarian organisations such as:

- United Nations
- European Union
- The Red Cross
- BBC

Whatever their rationale, organisations that work in the international domain must have an extremely well-honed sense of diplomacy. They work with cultures that have different norms, different styles, values and beliefs. Bridging these divides whilst working to a common end is not always easy.

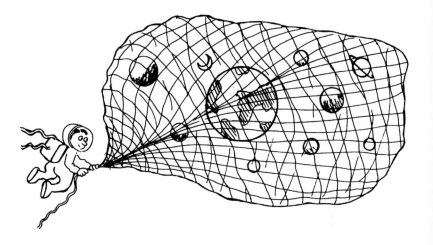

Appropriateness is vital, sensitivity and understanding essential. Nothing can be taken for granted. The mere interpretation of words can be a stumbling block in what may seem the most innocuous of circumstances.

International organisations have been significant in bringing together cultures from every corner of the globe to work to a common end. In this way, the concept of the global village becomes a reality.

Strategic networks are a very different concept. As a manager, you will be only too aware of strategy. You probably have a role in the creation, development and implementation of it. In addition, you will have an understanding of networks. This will not only be from reading this book but from other sources of information, tacit or explicit. So, how do strategy and networks come together?

Strategic networks

Strategic networks are clusters of organisations that cooperate with each other in pursuit of a common goal. Simplistically speaking, strategic networks are primarily concerned with their customers, people with whom it is essential to build effective long-term relationships.

Networks are ideally suited to this activity. In order to build a successful network, it is important to examine the interests of various parties and address different business factors. These include:

Human perspective	*Business perspective*
• Customer	• Market-place trends
• Stakeholders	• Politics
• Shareholders	• Economy
• Suppliers/contractors	• Financial viability
• Values and beliefs	• Organisational skill set
• Culture	

It is the mix of these factors that makes organisations unique.

To help you understand strategic networks, we will look back to how they have evolved. An organism evolves from a combination of cross-fertilisation and development. Strategic networks are no different. They have evolved as a result of combining the most successful features of different types of organisations: vertically integrated organisations and fully disintegrated organisations (sometimes known as strategic alliances).

Vertically integrated organisations
A vertically integrated organisation is one that retains responsibility for everything from resourcing to marketing (in the case of General Motors, from smelting to the final polish). In the current business environment, vertically integrated organisations have emerged as inflexible, cumbersome structures and ones that are extremely expensive to run.

Vertically integrated organisations can be clearly identified by their features:

- Hierarchical
- Clearly defined roles and responsibilities
- Individual accountability and reward
- Mapped successions
- Set methods and procedures
- Clear systems and processes
- Processes defined and enforced
- Inward-looking
- Self-contained

Due to the bureaucratic nature of the vertically integrated organisation, it is extremely difficult to build up the momentum for change, now a constant component of the business world.

Some of the more significant aspects of vertically integrated organisations are expanded below. These include:

- Focus
- Analysis versus synthesis
- Control

Focus   The focus in these organisations is on the product or product line. Less emphasis is placed on the customer or on an understanding of the market and the way it is, or may be, developing.

This tendency to be blinkered can have disastrous consequences and many giants in the market have fallen because of this inward-looking, self-contained approach. The Swiss watchmakers were a case in point, underrating the impact that quartz technology would have on the clockwork industry. IBM have teetered on this brink too and have had to embark on massive change initiatives in order to survive.

Analysis versus synthesis   In vertically integrated organisations, actions are taken and goals are set on the basis of analysis: sales, costs, markets, competition. This is only part of the story though and good decisions often go bad because the focus of the analysis is too small and draws the logic towards the wrong conclusions.

If the flow of information was better in these structures, a higher level of analysis would result: synthesis. In this sense, a cooperative exchange of information would take place with those who have a different perspective on the issue and the various inputs synthesised to create a broad-based understanding.

Control   On the more positive side, vertically integrated organisations have complete control over all the stages of manufacture and, when the product is in line with market forces, the rewards are excellent.

Fully disintegrated organisations

Fully disintegrated organisations, or strategic alliances, are at the opposite extreme to vertically integrated organisations. They consist of a group of organisations such as:

- Suppliers
- Manufacturers
- Contractors
- Consultants
- Agents

This group comes alongside a core organisation in order to contribute to the achievement of at least one business objective.

Each organisational grouping, comprising one or more strategic alliances, is managed by the core, which subcontracts elements of the entire business process from conception to delivery, whilst avoiding the responsibility of the financial and operational health of the contributing organisation.

The organisations that form a strategic alliance with the core may well have formed other strategic alliances with different cores and, in these cases, will have other customers to satisfy. Organisations of this nature are sometimes referred to as 'virtual' organisations.

The reasons for operating through a set of strategic alliances are compelling but not all-embracing.

Positives The size and capability of organisations can be changed rapidly to meet market demands. Product lines can be changed or expanded relatively easily and manufacturers can be selected on the basis of their technological and economic superiority. The responsibility for research and development and the need to invest in new production processes can be avoided.

Negatives Although slim and inexpensive to run, however, one fairly large disadvantage with strategic alliances is that they present a real challenge in terms of their management. It is by no means easy to orchestrate a group of autonomous units with a complex set of motivations.

In addition, the core organisation can suffer from being remote from the innovators (suppliers and manufacturers), and from their customers, who may be serviced exclusively by franchisees. Second-hand, second-rate customer intelligence can thwart these organisations' attempts to respond quickly to changes in the market.

As the number of stakeholders in the network increases, so does the confusion of information and communication. It flows in all directions from many different sources. The messages that are transmitted and received in this way are not always accurate or helpful.

Alliance networks
Alliance networks are a cluster, or group, of organisations that join together in a mutually beneficial relationship. The members of the alliance may ebb and flow. The formality and strength of the links will also vary according to the group's objectives. Examples of alliance networks exist in the following industries:

- Computer
- Travel
- Automotive

By forming alliances, economies of scale can be achieved which facilitate procurement and build momentum in particular market sectors.

Alliance networks are made up of a number of different core organisations from the same industry who get together to dominate the market. They are not (technically speaking) dominated by one specific organisation.

Alliance networks have been responsible for the creation of international industry standards. Organisations within a common market unite in the promotion of specific standards until a critical mass is achieved. This swings the market in the direction of the agreed standard, pushing out those that have not managed to form a sufficiently strong alliance of competing organisations.

Strategic networks
As a result of the drawbacks of fully integrated and disintegrated organisations, a hybrid organisational structure has evolved. This is called a strategic network.

We will now view strategic networks from a number of different perspectives:

- Control
- Information
- Communication
- Market
- Trust
- Dangers

Control   In a strategic network, the core organisation controls, but does not own any of the contributing organisations. Instead, they are firmly tied into the management system. Indeed, they cannot exist in the same way outside this system because with it comes the 'organisational spirit' or brand image from which they profit.

Information   Harnessed well, the information exchanged within the boundaries of an organisation based on the principles of a strategic network can be extremely valuable.

Communication   The channels of communication facilitate the collection and distribution of information and encourage innovation from all staff. It is the task of management to bring together and synthesise information which will, in turn, lead to the best decision with regard to the organisation's strategic direction.

Market   This style of organisation has the added advantage of being able to get alongside its customer and really determine what is wanted in the market. Being close to the ground in this way has led to some remarkable successes. The international success of McDonald's and Benetton illustrates this clearly.

Trust   As with all styles of networking, trust is of paramount importance to successful strategic networking. In the strategic network, those linked to the core organisation have to be able to trust that their efforts are properly represented and rewarded through the ultimate success and reputation of the product.

Dangers   All systems have dangers.

In an ideal world, your contractors will feel a strong sense of affiliation and will demonstrate loyalty and commitment. In addition, they will work to your own set of standards and contribute, generally, to the culture of the organisation. Beware of sourcing from just one contractor as they can hold you hostage. No contractor is indispensable and it is extremely disruptive when your sole contractor withdraws from your operation with little warning. It takes time to identify alternatives and they will not be operating with full knowledge of your requirements, or at full speed, immediately.

Exceptional management skills are needed to ensure that the organisation's activities and culture are not fragmented or suffer from any wayward forces.

Opposite is a diagnostic tool to help you identify the characteristics of your own organisation or operation.

	Integrated	Strategic networks	Alliance networks	Strategic alliance
Structure	Monolithic Inflexible Internal suppliers	Entrepreneurial Responsive Exclusive subcontractors	Independent Individual Autonomous organisations	Disparate Uncoordinated Various subcontractors
Focus	Product	Customer	Global market	Market
Management	Bureaucratic	Flexible	Collective governance	Complex
Culture	Status-conscious	Culture-driven	Market leader	Brand-centred

The reason that strategic networks have emerged as the best organisational structure is that changes in the business environment, largely as a result of a worldwide recession, have forced organisations to look at how their structure can best assist their performance. Strategic networks seem to be able to combine flexibility and efficiency with low operating costs and high profitability.

This growing trend is highlighted when large fully vertically integrated organisations, such as Shell and GEC, divest themselves of specialist manufacturing operations or services and contract them back in on different terms. In addition, strategic alliances work hard to promote an organisational culture through the integration of technology, training, product awareness and communication.

Summary

Organisations dominate the world and they too benefit from their networks. Strategic networks determine:

- Focus
- Management style
- Culture
- Development
- Products
- Control
- Responsiveness
- Flexibility

■ F R I D A Y ■

Whatever your level within the organisation you will be
affected by strategic networks directly or indirectly.
Strategic networks will not only impact on your immediate
future and style of operation, but on your long-term future:
your career. Start by thinking strategically as an individual,
developing competencies and behaviours that will be
required by the new-style organisation.

Simple steps to networking success

Throughout the week we have given you a framework for understanding networks and networking. We began by looking at definitions and identifying themes. All commentators agree that networks are built on contacts; contacts at all levels: personal, professional, within organisations and between organisations. Whatever the level of the contact and the aim in establishing it, the overriding goal of networking is to build and manage productive relationships.

The primary responsibility for your network lies with you!

Today, we will help you take on this responsibility, by summarising the week's activities, reiterating some of the most important aspects of good networking and suggesting some habits that you could form. We have broken this down into five simple steps:

Step one   – Map your network
Step two   – Identify your style
Step three – Clarify your goals
Step four   – Develop networking behaviours
Step five   – Benefit

Step one: Map your network

We live and work within networks and yet most people are
unaware of them. This naïve ignorance will threaten the
survival of managers in the future. Living and working
with, through and in harmony with your network will
become a necessity. Successful managers will be judged on
the quality of their networks and their ability to manage
their networks effectively. The first step to success requires
that you understand who is in your network and where it
has its strongest potential.

Network, what network?
You need to own and recognise your network. The most
powerful way to understand your network is to see it. Take
a piece of flipchart paper (anything smaller will be too
small) and use an ordinary pen, not a marker, it will be too
big!

Mapping your network
1 Draw a circle with your name in it ('me' would do!)
2 Attach a stick to this circle – it will look like a lollipop
3 At the end of this stick draw another circle – it will
   now look like a set of dumb bells

4 Put the name of one of your primary networks in it –
professional, personal and so forth

5 Add more such sticks until you have what looks like
a daisy

6 For each circle in your network tree, add more
lollipops – put contact names and telephone
numbers in them

7 If one contact was given to you by another – link
these together like a chain

8 Note the overlaps between networks – they often
interlink

Don't be too fussy about how your map develops, nobody
else needs to understand it.

When you have completed your map with as many names
as you can, stand back and look at it. Who have you
forgotten? On Sunday, we gave you a list of potential
network contacts. Have you included friends and
acquaintances, family, school friends and teachers, college
friends and lecturers, community and council leaders,
church, parish and religious leaders, doctors and dentists,
sports, leisure or social club members, members of institutes
and associations, former employers, peers from previous
jobs, bosses, colleagues, customers, consultants, suppliers,
competitors, contractors, agents and distributors? Add any
omissions to your map.

Your map will be constantly changing in accordance with
your needs, goals, exposure and experiences.

Support your map with information. You may want to use
the contact record form we referred to on Thursday. There

are also a number of computer packages that help you to
organise this kind of information, everything from the Lotus
Organiser to specially adapted contact management
software. Keep snippets of information on your records too.
It is such an advantage to be able to open your conversation
with a contact with a question such as:

How's your daughter doing at University?
Was your trip to The States a success?

or some other *uncontentious* question! Always keep your
records up to date and in a form to which you can add
simply.

Step two: Identify your style

Your map is a tangible illustration of where you have made
your investment. To balance this picture you need to reflect
on your style. Attempt to answer the following question
honestly:

What is your networking style?

You may need to look to the past to give you an indication
of your style. Do you:

- Like meeting new people?
- Feel happiest focused on a task or in a group?
- Take opportunities to move in new circles?
- Create opportunities to enhance your visibility?
- Develop contacts in a wide variety of groups?
- Stay in close contact with your customers or clients?
- Enjoy meetings, training courses and conferences?
- Know and talk to peers in other organisations?

Your answers to the above questions will give you a clue to your preferred style.

On Sunday, we suggested three styles: conscious, intuitive and open.

Conscious networkers have clear goals; they recognise the gaps in their network, identify opportunities to explore and the people to fill the gaps.

Intuitive networkers feel happiest surrounded by people. They find themselves networking with everyone from their milkman to their children.

Open networkers invest in networks for their future potential. Translating such a network into something that is focused and can deliver the goods may be a stumbling block for open networkers.

Networking isn't something that everyone feels comfortable with immediately. If the thought of being surrounded by people brings you out in a cold sweat, fills you with dread or immediately raises your anxiety level, you will need to develop your skills consciously through scripting, rehearsing and practice. It is not necessarily true that you don't have the ability to network, you have probably never had the opportunity to practise and develop your skills.

Step three: Clarify your goals

The planning is now complete for your journey. However, to be a successful networker you need to have a destination in mind. Once you have established your destination it is easier to monitor your progress as you journey along your route. This requires action: establishing, maintaining, nurturing and pruning networks.

What is your destination?
We introduced models on Sunday which we have referred to throughout the week. Networks are for:

- Information
- Development
- Support
- Influence

Information
Managers need to keep up to date. To do this, a large amount of personal commitment, time and energy is required. To help you in this process you need access to hubs and informers:

- Hubs
  - influential sources of information
  - suggest helpful connections
- Informers
  - provide new approaches and perspectives
  - recognise problems and opportunities
  - understand market trends and developments

Be sure to choose your people well. Ensure that you consult with a variety of sources to get a balanced picture.

Development

A manager who isn't developing isn't performing. Don't assume that development is solely gained through training. You develop in many other ways: meetings, new projects, secondments, visits, seminars, reviews etc. It is important to ask yourself constantly, 'How could I improve?' You should also ask this of others. Approach:

- Experts
  - those who are respected and valued
  - the people you would recommend to others
- Challengers
  - cause you to look at your own direction
  - ask key questions about your life

Seeking and receiving feedback openly and regularly creates a natural environment for development.

Support

No manager is an island. You need people to support you and to sponsor your entry into new networks. This will enable you to maintain and develop your networks. Ask yourself, 'Who should I surround myself with?'

- Foundations
  - on whom we depend
- Sounding boards
  - hold you in the highest esteem
  - give you time
- Sherpas
  - help you achieve objectives
  - offer practical help and support

Never underestimate the value of support. It can often go unrecognised until it's removed.

Influence

All managers need help along the way – people who can make things happen, endorse a project, open doors and give you career guidance. Don't restrict yourself to just one person – seek influential people within your organisation or your profession. Ask yourself, 'Who could help me in the short and long term?'

- Resourcers
  - support you with resources
  - believe in your ideas
- Mentors
  - guide your career
  - teach you the ropes

- Promoters
  - advise you of opportunities
  - encourage your visibility

Don't be afraid to ask. It can be flattering to be asked to fulfil an influencing role – people can always say no!

Planning your route
In planning your route you first have to refer to your map. Are there any road blocks? Do you have restricted access to information, development, support or influence?

Asking yourself this question will give you an indication of where you need to:

- Invest
- Hold
- Prune

Invest   Which relationships warrant investment currently? Which networks have you neglected?

- Personal
- Organisational
- Professional
- Strategic

Which network could help you achieve your goal? If you have already decided what you want to achieve, you can probably identify the person who can help or support you in your endeavours. If this person is not immediately identifiable, think of how you might write a job advertisement specifying the type of person who could do it. You may recognise them as being inside one of your networks already.

You may decide to invest in the networks that you want to maintain, or you may have identified gaps in your network that are critical.

Who could bridge the gap?

It is these issues which require investment.

Hold   It may be that you have networks that, whilst important, require little special attention or effort. These are the networks which you can access at any point and personal investment is not always necessary. It could be that they are well developed or that others within them maintain them.

Prune   Which networks aren't so critical or important? You could choose to spend less time and energy on these. Decisions to prune networks are always difficult and can seem callous and calculating.

To have the energy to invest in new networks, you need to be realistic about those that are not serving you well and, where necessary, withdraw from them.

Too many plans fail because the goal is not clear enough. Be clear in your goals and plan your route towards them. Always remember that plans may need to change as your circumstances change.

Regularly review your progress by asking yourself:

What do I want from my network?
What am I prepared to contribute?

Your answers will keep you on the road to success.

Telling somebody about your plan is a good way of making your plan into a contract and ensuring that you stick to it. Also, hearing yourself saying things out loud and seeing others' reactions to what you say brings a new understanding and clarity. Choose your sounding board with care on the basis of their experience, skills and the quality of your relationship. This is a great way to start developing your networking skills and behaviours.

Step four: Develop networking behaviours

There is an unwritten code of ethics for good networking practice.

Networking behaviours
- Be open-minded
- Keep commitments

- Do as you would be done by
- Don't be afraid to ask
- Give without exception
- Say thank you

Many people are cynical about networking as an activity. They see it as taking advantage of people's goodwill for personal gain. This is not the case. We all have a natural sense of justice; try and gauge what this is for each person you contact. People will not cooperate if they feel that there is nothing in it for them. They very quickly get tired of giving and will soon stop. Networking therefore contains its own control system.

The best approach is *'do as you would be done by'*. In this way, you can put yourself in the other person's shoes and ask yourself whether your demands are reasonable. If you think you are stretching your credibility a bit, you might like to think of what incentives or rewards would balance the books.

Remember you are a part of others' networks:

- Keep your eyes and ears open
- Open doors
- Refer and recommend
- Publicise their achievements
- Suggest projects

Step five: Benefit

Networking is here to stay. So, if you want to:

- Ensure balance
- Create visibility
- Increase employability

understand and invest in your networks.

Ensure balance
Balance is hard to maintain. This is particularly true these days because of the complex dynamics of life. Networks can help you in the following ways:

> *Balance*
>
> support – challenge
> doing – thinking
> personal – professional

By constantly monitoring and managing your networks you can ensure a state of equilibrium is achieved.

Create visibility
Many large organisations today can be very impersonal. It is easy to get lost in the crowd. If you know how to network and how to identify the hubs and sponsors, people will get to know you.

Outside your organisation, networks are fascinating. Once you begin networking you will realise what a small world it is.

Ensure employability
You can ensure employability by:

- Building networks with integrity
- Bridging the gaps

Building networks with integrity   Prospective employers may be interested in you solely because of your network. Professionals such as stockbrokers, advertisers, sales people, editors and consultants have key contacts and have developed strong relationships. Often these contacts offer their allegiance to the individual rather than the organisation. Employers may judge you on the quality and loyalty of your network.

Bridging the gaps   Successful people know that the way to good opportunities and advancement can come from a network that is carefully maintained.

Summary

To do anything well requires focused attention and effort and networking is no exception. These simple steps show that it is not something to be done haphazardly. Your time is far too valuable to be wasted in that way.

- Know
- Develop
- Mobilise

your network; you will then be able to enjoy the rewards.

It cannot be stressed enough, networking is a highly valuable activity. It holds rewards for all parties if managed conscientiously. Have fun with your networks but use them prudently, and good luck! With new 'networking eyes' you will see life's possibilities in a new light.